Corsons Inlet

CORSONS INLET

A Book of Poems

A. R. AMMONS

Cornell University Press   ITHACA, NEW YORK

CORNELL UNIVERSITY PRESS

First published 1965
Second printing 1966

Library of Congress Catalog Card Number: 65-13126

PRINTED IN THE UNITED STATES OF AMERICA
BY SCIENCE PRESS, INC.
BOUND BY VAIL-BALLOU PRESS, INC.

for Family, for Friends

ACKNOWLEDGMENTS

Grateful acknowledgment is made to the editors of the following publications for permission to reprint the poems listed:

Accent, for "Driving Through," "Ritual for Eating the World," "Thaw," "Two Hymns," and "Whose Timeless Reach"; *Chelsea*, for "Motion"; *Chicago Review*, for "Anxiety" and "Four Motions for the Pea Vines"; *Compass Review*, for "The Wide Land"; *Discourse*, for "Jungle Knot" and "Prodigal"; *Epoch*, for "Butterflyweed," "Coon Song," "Dunes," "Lines," "Moment," "Resort," "Upright," and "Winter Scene."

Hudson Review, for "Corsons Inlet" (formerly "A Nature Walk"), "Open," and "The Watch"; *The Nation*, for "Portrait" and "Visit"; *The New York Times*, for "Loss" and "Spindle"; *Partisan Review*, for "March Song"; *Poetry*, for "Catalyst," "Dark Song," "Epiphany," "Gravelly Run," "Street Song," and "World"; *Quarterly Review of Literature*, for "Glass," "Libation," and "The Strait"; *Shenandoah*, for "The Yucca Moth."

The poems "Loss" and "Spindle" © 1964 by The New York Times Company. Reprinted by permission.

CONTENTS

Corsons Inlet

Visit

It is not far to my place:
you can come smallboat,
pausing under shade in the eddies
  or going ashore
    to rest, regard the leaves

  or talk with birds and
shore weeds: hire a full-grown man not
late in years to oar you
  and choose a canoe-like thin ship;
    (a dumb man is better and no

  costlier; he will attract
the reflections and silences under leaves:)
travel light: a single book, some twine:
  the river is muscled at rapids with trout
    and a laurel limb

  will make a suitable spit: if you
leave in the forenoon, you will arrive
with plenty of light
  the afternoon of the third day: I will
    come down to the landing

  (tell your man to look for it,
the dumb have clear sight and are free of
visions) to greet you with some made
  wine and a special verse:
    or you can come by shore:

  choose the right: there the rocks
cascade less frequently, the grade more gradual:
treat yourself gently: the ascent thins both
  mind and blood and you must
    keep still a dense reserve

1

of silence we can poise against
conversation: there is little news:
I found last month a root with shape and
have heard a new sound among
the insects: come.

Moment

He turned and
stood

in the moment's
height,

exhilaration
sucking him up,

shuddering and
lifting

him
jaw and bone

and he said
what

destruction am I
blessed by?

Winter Scene

There is now not a single
leaf on the cherry tree:

except when the jay
plummets in, lights, and,

in pure clarity, squalls:
then every branch

quivers and
breaks out in blue leaves.

Corsons Inlet

I went for a walk over the dunes again this morning
to the sea,
then turned right along
    the surf
               rounded a naked headland
               and returned

    along the inlet shore:

it was muggy sunny, the wind from the sea steady and high,
crisp in the running sand,
    some breakthroughs of sun
  but after a bit

continuous overcast:

the walk liberating, I was released from forms,
from the perpendiculars,
    straight lines, blocks, boxes, binds
of thought
into the hues, shadings, rises, flowing bends and blends
        of sight:

                  I allow myself eddies of meaning:
yield to a direction of significance
running
like a stream through the geography of my work:
    you can find
in my sayings
            swerves of action
            like the inlet's cutting edge:
        there are dunes of motion,
organizations of grass, white sandy paths of remembrance
in the overall wandering of mirroring mind:

but Overall is beyond me: is the sum of these events

I cannot draw, the ledger I cannot keep, the accounting
beyond the account:

in nature there are few sharp lines: there are areas of
primrose
        more or less dispersed;
disorderly orders of bayberry; between the rows
of dunes,
irregular swamps of reeds,
though not reeds alone, but grass, bayberry, yarrow, all . . .
predominantly reeds:

I have reached no conclusions, have erected no boundaries,
shutting out and shutting in, separating inside
        from outside: I have
        drawn no lines:
        as

manifold events of sand
change the dune's shape that will not be the same shape
tomorrow,

so I am willing to go along, to accept
the becoming
thought, to stake off no beginnings or ends, establish
        no walls:

by transitions the land falls from grassy dunes to creek
to undercreek: but there are no lines, though
        change in that transition is clear
        as any sharpness: but "sharpness" spread out,
allowed to occur over a wider range
than mental lines can keep:

the moon was full last night: today, low tide was low:
black shoals of mussels exposed to the risk
of air
and, earlier, of sun,
waved in and out with the waterline, waterline inexact,

caught always in the event of change:
>a young mottled gull stood free on the shoals
>and ate
to vomiting: another gull, squawking possession, cracked a crab,
picked out the entrails, swallowed the soft-shelled legs, a ruddy
turnstone running in to snatch leftover bits:

risk is full: every living thing in
siege: the demand is life, to keep life: the small
white blacklegged egret, how beautiful, quietly stalks and spears
>the shallows, darts to shore
>>to stab—what? I couldn't
>see against the black mudflats—a frightened
>fiddler crab?

>the news to my left over the dunes and
reeds and bayberry clumps was
>>fall: thousands of tree swallows
>>gathering for flight:
>>an order held
>>in constant change: a congregation
rich with entropy: nevertheless, separable, noticeable
>>as one event,
>>>not chaos: preparations for
flight from winter,
cheet, cheet, cheet, cheet, wings rifling the green clumps,
beaks
at the bayberries:
>a perception full of wind, flight, curve,
>sound:
>the possibility of rule as the sum of rulelessness:
the "field" of action
with moving, incalculable center:

in the smaller view, order tight with shape:
blue tiny flowers on a leafless weed: carapace of crab:
snail shell:

7

pulsations of order
in the bellies of minnows: orders swallowed,
broken down, transferred through membranes
to strengthen larger orders: but in the large view, no
lines or changeless shapes: the working in and out, together
and against, of millions of events: this,
so that I make
no form of
formlessness:

orders as summaries, as outcomes of actions override
or in some way result, not predictably (seeing me gain
the top of a dune,
the swallows
could take flight—some other fields of bayberry
could enter fall
berryless) and there is serenity:

no arranged terror: no forcing of image, plan,
or thought:
no propaganda, no humbling of reality to precept:

terror pervades but is not arranged, all possibilities
of escape open: no route shut, except in
the sudden loss of all routes:

I see narrow orders, limited tightness, but will
not run to that easy victory:
still around the looser, wider forces work:
I will try
to fasten into order enlarging grasps of disorder, widening
scope, but enjoying the freedom that
Scope eludes my grasp, that there is no finality of vision,
that I have perceived nothing completely,
that tomorrow a new walk is a new walk.

Dunes

Taking root in windy sand
    is not an easy
way
to go about
    finding a place to stay.

A ditchbank or wood's edge
    has firmer ground.

In a loose world though
    something can be started —
a root touch water,
    a tip break sand —

Mounds from that can rise
    on held mounds,
a gesture of building, keeping,
    a trapping
into shape.

Firm ground is not available ground.

Street Song

Like an
eddying willow leaf
I stand

on the street
and turn:
people,

both ways coming
and going
around me, swirl:

probably I
am no stiller—
detached; but

gold is
coming
into my veins.

Lines

Lines flying in, out: logarithmic
    curves coiling
toward an infinitely inward center: lines
    weaving in, threads lost in clustral scrawl,
    weaving out into loose ends,
wandering beyond the border of gray background,
    going out of vision,
    not returning;
or, returning, breaking across the boundary
    as new lines, discontinuous,
    come into sight:
fiddleheads of ferns, croziers of violins,
    convoluted spherical masses, breaking through
    ditchbanks where briar
stem-dull will
    leave and bloom:
    haunch line, sickle-like, turning down, bulging, nuzzling
under, closing into
    the hidden, sweet, dark meeting of lips:
    the spiraling out
or in
    of galaxies:
    the free-running wavy line, swirling
configuration, halting into a knot
    of curve and density: the broken,
    irreparable filament: tree-winding vines, branching,
falling off or back, free,
    the adventitious preparation for possibility, from
    branch to branch, ash to gum:
the breaker
    hurling into reach for shape, crashing
    out of order, the inner hollow sizzling flat:
the longnecked, uteral gourd, bass line

continuous in curve,
   melodic line filling and thinning:
concentrations,
   whirling masses,
      thin leaders, disordered ends and risks:
explosions of clusters, expansions from the
   full radial sphere, return's longest chance:
      lines exploring, intersecting, paralleling, twisting,
noding: deranging, clustering.

Coon Song

I got one good look
    in the raccoon's eyes
        when he fell from the tree
came to his feet
    and perfectly still
        seized the baying hounds
in his dull fierce stare,
    in that recognition all
    decision lost,
choice irrelevant, before the
    battle fell
    and the unwinding
of his little knot of time began:

        Dostoevsky would think
it important if the coon
    could choose to
        be back up the tree:
or if he could choose to be
    wagging by a swamp pond,
        dabbling at scuttling
crawdads: the coon may have
    dreamed in fact of curling
        into the holed-out gall
of a fallen oak some squirrel
    had once brought
        high into the air
clean leaves to: but

        reality can go to hell
is what the coon's eyes said to me:
    and said how simple
        the solution to my
problem is: it needs only

not to be: I thought the raccoon
        felt no anger,
saw none; cared nothing for cowardice,
        bravery; was in fact
        bored at
knowing what would ensue:
        the unwinding, the whirling growls,
        exposed tenders,
the wet teeth—a problem to be
        solved, the taut-coiled vigor
        of the hunt
ready to snap loose:

        you want to know what happened,
you want to hear me describe it,
        to placate the hound's-mouth
        slobbering in your own heart:
I will not tell you: actually the coon
        possessing secret knowledge
        pawed dust on the dogs
and they disappeared, yapping into
        nothingness, and the coon went
        down to the pond
and washed his face and hands and beheld
        the world: maybe he didn't:
        I am no slave that I
should entertain you, say what you want
        to hear, let you wallow in
        your silt: one two three four five:
one two three four five six seven eight nine ten:
        (all this time I've been
        counting spaces
while you were thinking of something else)
        mess in your own sloppy silt:
        the hounds disappeared
yelping (the way you would at extinction)

into—the order
breaks up here—immortality:
I know that's where you think the brave
little victims should go:
I do not care what
you think: I do not care what you think:
I do not care what you
think: one two three four five
six seven eight nine ten: here we go
round the here-we-go-round, the
here-we-go-round, the here-we-
go-round: coon will end in disorder at the
teeth of hounds: the situation
will get him:
spheres roll, cubes stay put: now there
one two three four five
are two philosophies:
here we go round the mouth-wet of hounds:

what I choose
is youse:
baby

Portrait

Dry-leaf life
curls up on
lobe toes

and like a lost
or haunted crab
skitters

across the street,
fretting at
the wind,

or curled forward
tumbles down or
even up a

rise, gay and
light as a
spring catkin,

or boatlike strikes
a stream or, wet,
flattens

out stream-bottom
in windless
black: come,

wind, away from
water and let
song spring &

leap with this
paper-life's
lively show.

Jungle Knot

One morning Beebe
    found on a bank of the Amazon
an owl and snake
    dead in a coiled embrace:

    the vine prints its coil too deep into the tree
and leaved fire shoots greens of tender flame
    rising among the branches,
drawing behind a hardening, wooden clasp:

the tree does not
    generally escape
though it may live thralled for years,
    succumbing finally rather than at once,

    in the vine's victory
the casting of its eventual death,
    though it may live years
on the skeletal trunk,

termites rising, the rain softening,
    a limb in storm
falling, the vine air-free at last, structureless as death:
    the owl,

    Beebe says, underestimated
the anaconda's size: hunger had deformed
    sight or caution, or
anaconda, come out in moonlight on the river bank,

had left half his length in shade: (you
    sometimes tackle
more than just what the light shows):
    the owl struck talons

    back of the anaconda's head
but weight grounded him in surprise: the anaconda

17

coiled, embracing heaving wings
and cry, and the talons, squeezed in, sank

killing snake and owl in tightened pain:
errors of vision, errors of self-defense!
errors of wisdom, errors of desire!
the vulture dives, unlocks four eyes.

Dark Song

Sorrow how high it is
that no wall holds it
back: deep

it is that no dam undermines
it: wide that it
comes on as up a strand

multiple and relentless:
the young that are
beautiful must die; the

old, departing,
can confer
nothing.

Resort

Beautiful nature,
say
the neuter lovers

escaping
man/woman nature,
man

fierce competitive,
woman
taunting

treacherous:
regenerative nature,
they say

fingering the cool
red-dotted lichen
on an old

water-holding
stump:
sweet neutrality,

a calm love where
man and woman
are fang & fury.

Upright

He said
I am mud
in a universe of stone and fire,

neither hard
enough to last
nor expressed
    in one
of those imperishable fires.

Be something
the grassblade said
rising whitegreen

from common swamp.
I am he
said

nothing &
feel better that
way.

The grassblade
said
be like us

grass stone
and fire and
pass.

Mud is
nothing
and eternal.

Catalyst

Honor the maggot,
supreme catalyst:
he spurs the rate of change:
(all scavengers are honorable: I love them
all,
will scribble hard as I can for them)

he accelerates change
in the changeless continuum;
where the body falls completed, he sets to work:
where the spirit attains
indifference
he makes his residence:
in the egg on wing from mound
to mound he travels,
feeds, finds his wings,

after the wet-sweet of decay,
after the ant-sucked earth has drunk
the honey-fluids,
after
the veins
lie dried to streaks of tendon
inside the meat-free, illuminated skull,

lofts, saws the air, copulates in a hung
rapture
of riding, holds the sweet-clear
connection
through dual flights, male and female,
soil's victory:
(dead cell dross transfigured
into gloss,
iridescence of complex eyes,

duck-neck purple of hairy abdomen)

O worm supreme,
transformer of bloated, breaking flesh
into colorless netted wings,
into the wills of sex and song, leaving
ash on odorless ground, the scent
of pinestraw
rising dominant from the striking sun!

Loss

When the sun
falls behind the sumac
thicket the
wild
yellow daisies
in diffuse evening shade
lose their
rigorous attention
and
half-wild with loss
turn
any way the wind does
and lift their
petals up
to float
off their stems
and go

World

Breakers at high tide shoot
spray over the jetty boulders
that collects in shallow chips, depressions,

evening the surface to run-off level:
of these possible worlds of held water,
most can't outlast the interim tideless

drought, so are clear, sterile, encased with
salt: one in particular, though, a hole,
providing depth with little surface,

keeps water through the hottest day:
a slime of green algae extends into that
tiny sea, and animals tiny enough to be in a

world there breed and dart and breathe and
die: so we are here in this plant-created oxygen,
drinking this sweet rain, consuming this green.

Butterflyweed

The butterfly that
named the weed
drank there, Monarch,
scrolled, medallioned—
his wings lifted close
in pale underwing salute

occasionally would
with tense evenness
open down

hinged coffers
lawned against the sun:
anchored in
dream, I could hardly
fall when earth
dropped and looped away.

Configurations

1

when November stripped
    the shrub,
          what stood
          out
in revealed space was
a nest
    hung
    in essential limbs

2

    how harmless truth
    is
    in cold weather
    to an empty nest

3

dry
leaves
in
the
bowl,
        like wings

4

    summer turned light
    into darkness
    and inside the shadeful
    shrub
        the secret
        worked

itself into life:

icicles and waterpanes:
recognitions:

      at the bottom, knowledges
      and desertions

5

speech comes out,
      a bleached form,
nestlike:

      after the events of silence
      the flying away
    of silence
    into speech—

6

      the nest is held
      off-earth
by sticks;

      so, intelligence
      stays
      out of the ground

erect on a
brittle walk of bones:

      otherwise
      the sea,

      empty of separations

7

leaves
like wings
in the Nov

ember nest:

wonder where the birds are now that were here:
wonder if the hawks missed them:
wonder if
       dry wings
        lie abandoned,
      bodiless
      this
      November:

      leaves—   out of so many
                     a nestful missed the ground

8

I am a bush
I am a nest
I am a bird
I am a wind
I am a negg

    I is a bush, nest, bird, wind, negg
    I is a leaf

if I fall what falls:
the leaves fell and the birds flew away and winter came and

9

when
I
am   bringing
singing   those   home
'   two   again
summer birds
comes
back

so what if
lots of

        unfathomable stuff
        remains,
        inconceivable distances,

        closed and open infinities:
so what if
all that, if

        thunderstorms spill the eggs,
        loosen the nest, strew it across
        galaxies of grass and weeds:

who cares what remains when
only the interior
        immaterial
        configuration—

        shape—
        mattered, matters, immaterial, unremaining

11

there is some relationship between
proximity
to the earth and permanence:

        a shrub puts itself into and out of
        the earth at once,
earth and air united by a stem's
polar meshes of roots and branches:

        earth
        shrub
        nest
        leaf

                              bird

        the bird is somewhere south, unoriented
            to these roots:
        the leaves
                though they may not have wandered so far
            are random:

                        earth
                        shrub
                        nest

        goodbye, nest, if wind lifts you loose
        goodbye, shrub, if ice breaks you down
        goodbye,
        goodbye

        12

        the shrub is nothing
                except part of my song:
        the bird I never saw is part of my song and
                nothing else:

        (the leaves are a great many little notes I lost
            when I was trying to make the song
                that became my silence)

        13

        the cockbird longs for the henbird
        which longs for the nest
                which longs for the shrub which
        longs for the earth
        which longs for the sun which longs for

        14

        inside there the woodmeat is saying
                    please, please
                        let me put on my leaves

                         31

let me let the sap go

but the zero bark is saying
hush, hush
the time is not right
it's not the right time

the woodmeat is always right
but bark is knowing

Glass

The song
sparrow puts all his
saying
into one
repeated song:
what

variations, subtleties
he manages,
to encompass denser
meanings, I'm
too coarse
to catch: it's

one song, an overreach
from which
all possibilities,
like filaments,
depend:
killing,

nesting, dying,
sun or cloud,
figure up
and become
song—simple, hard:
removed.

Morning Glory

Dew was
heavy
last night:

sun-up broke
beads
into running

water: under
over
and

against,
the mockingbird
fluffing

amorously
bathes
in leaves

The Strait

At the oracle
I found the
   god
though active
recalcitrant

unliteral as air:
the priestess
   writhed
and moaned
caught

in the anguish
of some
   perishable
event:
birds flew by:

the urns
hummed: the
   columns
glazed with
sun; on the

inside lit wet with
fire: another, not
   capable
of the inner
speech,

read the priestess
and said,
   "The
god wants honor,
desires in you

honor's attitude:
honor him and
    your
venture will
go well":

cannot, I said,
the god be
    more
specific? will
I honor

him? come again
safe to this
    grove?
the reader said,
"The

descent of the
god is
    awkward,
narrowing and
difficult; first

he is
loose in the
    air,
then captured,
held, by

holy fire: the
circle of columns
    binds
him and from
the columns

the priestess
gathers him,
    seized

36

by her struggling
mouth into

a speech of
forms: it is
    speech
few can read,
the god

violent to
overreach the
    definite:
why should
he, who is

all, commit
himself to the
    particular?
say himself
into less

than all? pressed
too far, he
    leaves
wounds that are
invisible: it

is only as
she becomes
    him
that the priestess
cannot be hurt

or can be hurt:
should she
    break
her human hold
and go too far

with him,
who could bring
      her
back, her eyes
lost to the

visible? step
by step into the
      actual,
truth descending
breaks,

reaches us as
fragmentation
      hardened
into words'':
but, I said, isn't

it convenient
the priestess is
      general
and inexact, merely
turning and wailing?

if the god fails
me, whom shall I
      blame?
her? you who may
have read her wrong?

and if all goes
well, whom shall I
      thank?
the god
with honor,

you with the
actual coin?
      ''Night

falls," the reader said,
"the priestess lies

god-torn, limp: the
freed god
   flies
again blameless as
air: go

to your fate:
if you succeed, praise the
   god:
if you fail,
discover your flaw."

Spindle

This song is a violence
of icicles and
    windy trees:

rising it catches up
indifferent
    cellophane, loose

leaves, all mobiles
into an organized whirl
    relating scrap

to scrap in a round
fury: this violence
    brocades

the rocks with hard silver
of sea water and
    makes the tree

show the power of its
holding on: violence to make
    that can destroy.

The Yucca Moth

The yucca clump
        is blooming,
tall sturdy spears
        spangling into bells of light,
green
        in the white blooms
faint as a memory of mint:

I raid
        a bloom,
spread the hung petals out,
        and, surprised he's not
a bloom-part, find
        a moth inside, the exact color,
the bloom his daylight port or cove:

though time comes
        and goes and troubles
are unlessened,
        the yucca is lifting temples
of bloom: from the night
        of our dark flights, can
we go in to heal, live
        out in white-green shade
the radiant, white, hanging day?

Anxiety

The sparrowhawk
flies hard to

stand in the
air: something

about direction
lets us loose

into ease
and slow grace

Four Motions for the Pea Vines

I

the rhythm is
    diffusion and concentration:
in and out:
        expansion and
contraction: the unfolding,
    furling:

            the forces
            that propel the rhythm,
the lines of winding-up,
loosening, depositing,
    dissolving:

the vehicles!

light, the vehicle of itself, light
surrounding
we are made and fed by:
water, the solvent, vehicle
of molecules and grains,
the dissolver and depositor,
the maker of films
and residues,
the all-absorbing vessel uncontained!

            the rhythm is
            out and
            in,
            diffusion and concentration:

            the dry pea from the
            ground
            expands to vines and leaves,
            harvests sun and water

43

                    into
               baby-white new peas:

     the forms that exist
     in this rhythm! the whirling
          forms!
          grief and glory of
     this rhythm:
     the rhythm is

     2

     for the expansions (and concentrations) here
     is the five-acre
          Todd Field:

     seeding, too, is gathering,
     preparation to collect
                    mineral, rain, and light, and
     between the corn-rows,
     the broadcast field peas
     fall into soft, laying-by soil:

          dry beads of concentration
                    covered by the moist
     general ground:

     and the general moisture, the rain's
     held shadow, softens, breaks
     down, swells
     and frees
                    the hard incipience that
     generalizes outward toward extension;
     the root reaching with gravity,
     the stalk opposing
     crazing through the black land upward to the light

3
fat and sassy
    the raucous crows
    along the wood's edge
    trouble the tops of
yellowing pines
    with points of dipping black;

cluster into groups
from summer,
    the younglings in their wings
poised,
careful,
    precise,

the dazed awkwardness of heavy nest birds
hardened lean into grace;

assemble along the edge of the field and
        begin winter talk,
remembrances of summer and separations,
    agree
    or disagree
        on a roost,
        the old birds more often silent,

calmer and more tolerant in their memory,
    wiser of dangers
  experienced or conceived,
  less inclined to play,
  irritable,
        but at times

exultant in pitched flight,
as if catching for a moment
  youth's inexperienced gladness, or as if
      feeling

over time and danger
   a triumph greater than innocent joy:

to turn aside and live with them
   would not seem
      much different—

each of us going into winter with gains and losses,
dry, light peas of concentration nearby
   (for a winter's gleaning)
      to expand warmth through us

4

slow as the pale low-arcing sun, the women move
   down windy rows of the autumn field:
the pea vines are dead:
cornstalks and peapods rattle in the dry bleach
   of cold:

the women glean remnant peas
   (too old to snap or shell) that
got past being green; shatter from skeletal vines
   handfuls of peapods, tan, light:

bent the slow women drag towsacks huge
   with peas, bulk but little
weight: a boy carries a sack on his
   shoulders to the end of the rows:
he stoops: the sack goes over his head

to the ground: he flails it with a tobacco stick,
   opens the sack, removes the husks, and
from sack to tub winnows
   dry hard crackling peas: rhythms reaching through
seasons, motions weaving in and out!

Two Hymns

I

So when the year had come full round
I rose
and went out to the naked mountain
to see
the single peachflower on the sprout

blooming through a side of ribs
   possibly a colt's
and I endured each petal separately
and moved in orisons with the sepals

I lay
   said the sprouting stump
in the path of Liberty

Tyranny though I said is very terrible
and sat down leeward of the blossom
   to be blessed
and was startled by
a lost circling bee

The large sun setting red I went
down to the stream
   and wading in
let your cold water run over my feet

II

In the hour of extreme

   importance

when clots thicken
in outlying limbs and

47

warmth retreats

to mourn
the thinning garrison of pulse

keep my tongue loose
to sing possible

   changes

that might redeem

might in iron phrases
     clang the skies

bells and my jangling eyes
ringing you in
     to claim me

shriven celebrant
your love's new-reasoned singer

   home

dead on arrival

Open

Exuberance: joy to the last
pained loss
    and hunger of air:
life open, not decided on,
though decided in death:

            the mind cannot be
rid
while it works
    of remembered genitals
beautiful, dank, pliant,

of canyons, brush hills, pastures, streets,
    unities and divisions,
meetings,

exact remembrance of liquid buttocks,
navel, ellipse of hand,

magnified territories of going down
and rising,
    the thin tracing saliva line,

    joy's configurations:

serendipity: the unexpected,
the
possible, the unembodied,
        unevented:

the sun will burst: death
is certain: the future limited
    nevertheless is
limitless: the white knotted

    groin,

the finger describing
    entrances!

the dark, warm with glowing awareness, the
hot dis-
    missals of desire
until the last last tear of pain:

until the end nothing ends, lust
forward, rushing:
    pillars of ice wet-bright in melt,
warm

with always-yielding joy: yes
    yes
yes, the loose mouths hiss in the mornings of death.

Epiphany

Like a single drop of rain,
    the wasp strikes
the windowpane; buzzes rapidly
away, disguising

error in urgent business:
    such is the
invisible, hard as glass,
unrenderable by the senses,

not known until stricken by:
    some talk that
there is safety in the visible,
the definite, the heard and felt,

pre-stressing the rational and
    calling out with
joy, like people far from death:
how puzzled they will be when

going headlong secure in "things"
    they strike the
intangible and break, lost,
unaccustomed to transparency, to

being without body, energy
    without image:
how they will be dealt
hard realizations, opaque as death.

Prodigal

After the shifts and dis-
continuities, after the congregations of orders,
    black masses floating through
    mind's boreal clarity, icebergs in fog,
flotillas of wintering ducks weathering the night,
    chains of orders, multifilamentous chains
    knobbed with possibility, disoriented
chains, winding back on themselves, unwinding,
    intervolving, spinning, breaking off

    (nomads clustering at dusk into tents of sleep,
disorganizing, widening out again with morning)
    after the mental

    blaze and gleam,
the mind in both motions building and tearing down,
    running to link effective chains,
    establish molecules of meaning,
frameworks, to
    perfect modes of structuring
    (so days can bend to trellising
and pruned take shape,
    bloom into necessary event)

    after these motions, these vectors,
orders moving in and out of orders, collisions
    of orders, dispersions, the grasp weakens,

    the mind whirls, short of the unifying
reach, short of the heat
    to carry that forging:
    after the visions of these losses, the spent
seer, delivered to wastage, risen
    into ribs, consigns knowledge to
    approximation, order to the vehicle
of change, and fumbles blind in blunt innocence
    toward divine, terrible love.

Motion

The word is
not the thing:
is
a construction of,
a tag for,
the thing: the
word in
no way
resembles
the thing, except
as sound
resembles,
as in *whirr*,
sound:
the relation
between what this
as words
is
and what is
is tenuous: we
agree upon
this as the net to
cast on what
is: the finger
to
point with: the
method of
distinguishing,
defining, limiting:
poems
are fingers, methods,
nets,
not what is or

was:
but the music
in poems
is different,
points to nothing,
traps no
realities, takes
no game, but
by the motion of
its motion
resembles
what, moving, is—
the wind
underleaf white against
the tree.

The Misfit

The unassimilable fact leads us on:
round the edges
        where broken shapes make poor masonry
the synthesis
fails (and succeeds) into limitation
        or extending itself too far
becomes a different synthesis:
law applies
        consistently to the molecule,
not to the ocean, unoriented, unprocessed,
it floats in, that floats in it:
        we are led on

to the boundaries
where relations loosen into chaos
        or where the nucleus fails to control,
fragments in odd shapes
expressing more and more the interstitial sea:
        we are led on

to peripheries, to the raw blocks of material,
where mortar and trowel can convert
        diversity into enlarging unity:
not the million oriented facts
but the one or two facts,
        out of place,

recalcitrant, the one observed fact
that tears us into questioning:
        what has not
joined dies into order to redeem, with
loss of singleness extends the form,
        or, unassimilable, leads us on.

The Watch

When the sun went down and the night came on
coming over the fields and up the driveway
to the rose arbor and the backporch posts

I gathered myself together from dispersing dark
and went up into the mountains
and sitting down on the round rock beyond the trees

kindled my thoughts
blowing the coals of my day's bright conscious
and said

all across the plains my voice going silently and down
among the stumps where the swamp cuts through
and in between among the villages of hill country

Now close your eyes
Sleep
Shut out the world from the dark sweet freshening
    of your quiet hearts
Lie loose in the deep waters
Do not be afraid to
give yourselves up to drowning in undefended rest

If a dust storm blows up out of the west I will run
down the mountain and go through all the homes
and wake you up

If a new fire appears in the sky I will let you know
in time
so you can know it should it claim you

I will have all your beings in mind burning like a watchfire
and when the night has grown thin and weak
and the full coyotes have given up their calls

I will move up close to the eternal and
saying nine praises
commend you to it and to the coming sun

Libation

I have been throughout the world sleuthing,
drawing back goatheads
and from the writhing throats bloodletting,
watching the harassed religious eyes
whirl and freeze.

Earth drinks
the blood of fawns: jasmines
bloom in lions' eyes.

Breath and heat I have returned O Earth to your freedoms.
Now keep me virile and long at love:
let submission kiss off
the asking words from my lips.

The Wide Land

Having split up the chaparral
blasting my sight
the wind said
  You know I'm
    the result of
forces beyond my control
I don't hold it against you
I said
It's all right I understand

Those pressure bowls and cones
the wind said
are giants in their continental gaits
I know I said I know
they're blind giants
Actually the wind said I'm
  if anything beneficial
    resolving extremes
filling up lows with highs
No I said you don't have
to explain
It's just the way things are

Blind in the wide land I
turned and risked my feet
to loose stones and sudden

alterations of height

Thaw

Winter over, ice-bound
mind better not
rush to a spring-meet fast;
might trip, stiff thoughts,
    shatter:
better not warm up too
close to sun;
might melt, run, gullies
caking off the good
firm country of the brain.

Better go slow,
bend with the gradual movement,
let sap flow but
keep an eye on any
thermal swell rising at
    glassy mind.

If it gets loose wind
will take it
riddling through the underbrush,
but if it stays
solid brilliant ice
tulip root
    warm in coming
will splinter it.

Whose Timeless Reach

I Ezra the dying
portage of these deathless thoughts
stood on a hill in
the presence of the mountain
and said wisdom is
too wise for man it
is for gods and gods have little
use for it so I do not know what
to do with it
and animals use it only when
    their teeth start to fall and it
is too late to do anything
else but *be* wise and stay
out of the way
The eternal will not lie
down on any temporal hill
    The frozen mountain rose and broke
its tireless lecture of repose
and said death does
not take away it
ends giving halts bounty and
    Bounty I said thinking of ships
that I might take and helm right
· out through space
dwarfing these safe harbors and
their values
taking the Way in whose timeless reach
cool thought unpunishable
by bones eternally glides

Ritual for Eating the World

At a bend in the rocks there hung
inexplicably a rope
and musing I said
When I die don't bury me
under no weeping willer tree

It's I thought a hangman's loop
provided by my warmer ghoul to
raise me out of care

or god's own private fishing hook
for glaring people
who sit wasted in the sun
on rocks

But put me up in a high dry place
unavailable to the coyote's face

It's what I said old mountain
climbers left
dangling

The wind rides blade on mesa tops

Oh when I die don't bury me
under no weeping willer tree

and there being besides old bush
and distance nothing but a rope
I engaged myself with it but

it broke
and all through the heaving night
making day I faced

piecemeal the sordid
reacceptance of my world

Driving Through

In the desert midnight I said
taking out my notebook I
    am astonished
though widely traveled having
seen Empire State and Palestine, Texas
and San Miguel de Allende
to mention extremes
and sharpened my pencil on the sole
    of my shoe

The mountains running skidded
over the icy mirages of the moon
and fell down tumbling
    laughing for breath
on the cool dunes
The stone mosaics of the flattest
places (parting lake-gifts) grouped
    in colors and
played games at imagery: a green
tiger with orange eyes, an Orpheus
with moving fingers
    Fontal the shrubs flooded
everything with cool
water

I sat down against a brimming smoketree
to watch and morning found the
desert reserved
trembling at its hot and rainless task
    Driving through
you would never suspect
the midnight rite or seeing my lonely house
guess it will someday hold
laurel and a friend

March Song

At a bend in the stream by willows
I paused to be with the cattails
   their long flat leaves
and tall stems
bleached by wind and winter light

and winter had kept them
   edged down into the quiet eddy of the bend
tight with ice

O willows I said how you return
gold to the nakedness of your limbs
   coming again out of that country
into the longer sun

and Oh I said turning to the fluffy cattails
loosened to the approaching winds of spring
what a winter you leave in the pale stems
   of your becoming

Gravelly Run

I don't know somehow it seems sufficient
to see and hear whatever coming and going is,
losing the self to the victory
    of stones and trees,
of bending sandpit lakes, crescent
round groves of dwarf pine:

for it is not so much to know the self
as to know it as it is known
    by galaxy and cedar cone,
as if birth had never found it
and death could never end it:

the swamp's slow water comes
down Gravelly Run fanning the long
    stone-held algal
hair and narrowing roils between
the shoulders of the highway bridge:

holly grows on the banks in the woods there,
and the cedars' gothic-clustered
    spires could make
green religion in winter bones:

so I look and reflect, but the air's glass
jail seals each thing in its entity:

no use to make any philosophies here:
    I see no
god in the holly, hear no song from
the snowbroken weeds: Hegel is not the winter
yellow in the pines: the sunlight has never
heard of trees: surrendered self among
    unwelcoming forms: stranger,
hoist your burdens, get on down the road.